Food Dudes

HENRY JOHN HEINZ

Ketchup Developer

Heather C. Hudak

**Checkerboard
Library**

An Imprint of Abdo Publishing
www.abdopublishing.com

abdopublishing.com

Published by Abdo Publishing, a division of ABDO, PO Box 398166, Minneapolis, Minnesota 55439. Copyright © 2018 by Abdo Consulting Group, Inc. International copyrights reserved in all countries. No part of this book may be reproduced in any form without written permission from the publisher. Checkerboard Library™ is a trademark and logo of Abdo Publishing.

Printed in the United States of America, North Mankato, Minnesota
062017
092017

THIS BOOK CONTAINS
RECYCLED MATERIALS

Production: Mighty Media, Inc.
Editor: Liz Salzmann
Cover Photographs: Shutterstock (main), Wikimedia Commons (inset)
Interior Photographs: Alamy, pp. 17, 27; AP Images, p. 25; H.J. Heinz Company Photographs, MSP 57, Senator John Heinz History Center, pp. 9, 21; H.J. Heinz Company Records, MSS 57, Senator John Heinz History Center, p. 10; Library of Congress, pp. 8, 23; Shutterstock, pp. 5, 7, 13, 15, 24; Wikimedia Commons, pp. 1, 11, 19

Publisher's Cataloging-in-Publication Data

Names: Hudak, Heather C., 1975-, author.
Title: Henry John Heinz: ketchup developer / by Heather C. Hudak.
Other titles: Ketchup developer
Description: Minneapolis, MN : Abdo Publishing, 2018. | Series: Food dudes |
    Includes bibliographical references and index.
Identifiers: LCCN 2016962520 | ISBN 9781532110818 (lib. bdg.) |
    ISBN 9781680788662 (ebook)
Subjects: LCSH: Heinz, H. J. (Henry John), 1844--1919--Juvenile literature. | H.J.
    Heinz Company (Firm)--United States--Biography--Juvenile literature. |
    Businesspeople--United States--Biography--Juvenile literature.
Classification: DDC 641.6 [B]--dc23
LC record available at http://lccn.loc.gov/2016962520

Contents

Backyard Business

Today, Heinz ketchup is found in many restaurants in North America. Henry John Heinz introduced his brand of tomato ketchup in 1876. It has been the standard ever since.

Henry John "H.J." Heinz was born in Pittsburgh, Pennsylvania, on October 11, 1844. He was the oldest of eight children. H.J.'s parents, Anna Margaretha and John Henry Heinz, were German **immigrants**. When H.J. was six, the family moved to Sharpsburg, a village near Pittsburgh. There, his father ran a **brickyard**.

H.J.'s mother had a vegetable garden on the property. When not in school, H.J. helped his mother tend her garden. They grew more than enough for their family to eat. So, when H.J. was eight years old, he began selling the extra vegetables from the garden door-to-door.

In 1854, H.J.'s parents gave him his own small plot of land. He was able to grow and sell more vegetables. Soon he was able to buy more land for gardening. By the time he was 12 years old, H.J. had nearly 4 acres (1.6 ha) of land.

In 1854, H.J. helped make the bricks for the family home in Sharpsburg. In 1904, the house was moved to the Heinz plant in Pittsburgh. Since the 1950s, it has been in Dearborn, Michigan.

Horsing Around

It was clear from a young age that H.J. was a clever businessman. He continued to grow and sell vegetables, including horseradish. Horseradish is a root vegetable. It is often grated and used as a spice. But grating horseradish was difficult. To avoid the chore of grating, people would pay for grated horseradish. So, H.J. added grated horseradish to his products.

At the time, several companies sold grated horseradish. But H.J.'s product stood out from the competition. Companies didn't always wash the horseradish well before grating it. And they often added fillers such as turnips and wood shavings.

These companies packaged their horseradish in dark bottles to hide the dirt and fillers. H.J. used clear bottles so people could see how pure his product was. More and more people started choosing H.J.'s horseradish.

In addition to selling horseradish, H.J. also worked as a bookkeeper at his father's **brickyard**. Both of these jobs inspired him to learn more about business. So, H.J. attended Duff's Mercantile College in Pittsburgh.

Horseradish has a strong, spicy flavor. Grated horseradish is often mixed with vinegar to make a sauce.

Boom & Bust

Heinz and his wife, Sallie

In 1869, Heinz married Sarah Sloan Young, who went by the name Sallie. They would go on to have five children. That same year, Heinz started a business with his friend L. Clarence Noble.

The two men named the business Heinz, Noble & Company. It sold Heinz's horseradish. A few years later, the company added more products. These included pickles, **sauerkraut**, and vinegar.

For a while, business was booming. After the **American Civil War**, there was a period of growth and expansion across the country. People had enough

The bankruptcy was very upsetting for Heinz. He vowed to eventually pay everyone back.

money to buy the things they wanted and needed. And many of them were buying Heinz, Noble & Company's products.

Then in 1873, the **stock market** crashed. This caused an **economic** crisis that spread across the country. By 1875, more than 40 percent of people were out of work. Many companies were facing hard times, including Heinz and Noble's business.

Before the crash, Heinz, Noble & Company had purchased goods from suppliers on credit. After the crash, these suppliers asked the company to pay in full. And the banks demanded full payment for their loans. Heinz tried to raise enough money to save the company. But it was too late. The factory closed in December. On December 17, 1875, Heinz filed for **bankruptcy**.

Beginning Again

Heinz had reached rock bottom. His business had failed and he had no money. Many people were angry with him because he owed them money. But Heinz knew he could build a successful company again. However, the **bankruptcy** kept him from starting a new business. He was not legally allowed to own a company until he met certain requirements.

Heinz's mother, his brother John, and his cousin Frederick wanted to support his dream. They pooled what little money they had. In 1876, the family opened a business called the F. and J. Heinz Company. Heinz's wife sold some property she owned to buy a 50 percent **share** in the new business.

Heinz managed the company. He remembered the earlier success he had

One way F. and J. Heinz Company advertised its products was with printed catalogs.

Heinz continued to use clear bottles to show customers the quality of his products.

selling bottled horseradish. He realized that many people wanted affordable prepared foods. F. and J. Heinz Company filled this demand. Its products included horseradish, pickles, ketchup, and dressing.

Heinz bought a lot of advertisements to make buyers aware of his products. Soon, the company's products were being asked for in grocery stores across the nation. One product that was especially popular was ketchup. People had been making **versions** of this thick, seasoned sauce at home for hundreds of years. Now that they could buy it, it was flying out of the stores!

Ketchup History

Ketchup is a sauce that has been made of many things since the 1600s. Ingredients have included fish, walnuts, oysters, and mushrooms. Ketchup made from tomatoes became popular in the 1800s. Most people made their own ketchup. Some bought prepared ketchup that was imported from Great Britain. But this ketchup was expensive.

A big demand for affordable prepared ketchup in the United States developed. A few companies tried to fill this demand. These companies often added a lot of salt and **preservatives** to their ketchup recipes. These substances kept the ketchup from going bad. But they also made some people sick. The demand for an affordable, quality ketchup grew.

Heinz wanted to provide Americans with better ketchup at a lower price. He began with a ketchup based on his mother's recipe. Heinz ketchup was made with fresh tomatoes and no preservatives. It had more sugar, vinegar, and tomato **pulp** than other ketchups. Heinz ketchup also contained a special mix of spices. More and more people started buying Heinz ketchup.

Many of the first ketchup makers used tomato scraps leftover from canning tomatoes. Heinz was the first to start with whole, fresh tomatoes.

Advertising Genius

Sales of bottled ketchup helped the F. and J. Heinz Company grow quickly. Within ten years, Heinz was able to pay most of his earlier **debts**. This released him from **bankruptcy**. He could once again own a business.

By 1888, Heinz had bought both John's and Frederick's **shares** of the company. His mother suggested renaming the company. Heinz called his business the H.J. Heinz Company.

As the company's owner, Heinz continued to think up ways to advertise his products. He got one of his best ideas while visiting New York City. There, he saw a shoe store sign advertising "21 styles of shoes." He decided that Heinz company advertisements should also include a number.

Heinz chose the number 57, even though Heinz company had more than 60 products at the time. He just liked the number 57. It seemed like a lucky number to him. From then on, the Heinz company has used the **slogan**, "57 Varieties."

"57 Varieties" appears on nearly every Heinz company sign, label, and advertisement.

Keeping the Peace

With the success of his company, Heinz became known for strong business skills. He was also known for being a hard worker and a kind boss. This was due to his parents' influence. They taught their children to be generous and honest.

Heinz often rolled up his sleeves and went to work in the factory. He thought it was important to know how to do all parts of the business. He could be found doing everything from bottling products to putting labels on packages.

Quality was very important to Heinz. He wanted things done a certain way. He took the time to give workers guidance and advice. He also made the Heinz company factory a great place to work. It had a restaurant, a gym, showers, and a hospital.

People loved working for the Heinz company. In the late 1800s, it was common for factory workers to strike. They wanted better working conditions. But Heinz company workers were happy with their jobs. During Heinz's lifetime, H.J. Heinz Company employees never went on strike.

The Heinz factory had a garden on the roof. Workers could take their breaks there.

Boosting Business

While creating a quality workplace, Heinz also continued to look for ways to advertise. To this end, every Heinz bottle had a label with the company's logo on it. Heinz also put the logo on his delivery wagons. Billboards were another way he advertised.

Heinz took advantage of new opportunities to spread the word about his products. One of these was at the 1893 Chicago World's Fair. There, he set up a booth to show people his company's new methods of food processing.

At first, few people came to the Heinz booth. To encourage people to stop by, Heinz began offering **souvenirs**. It worked! Eventually, more than 1 million fairgoers visited the booth. Each received a charm shaped like a pickle.

In 1898, Heinz thought of yet another way to interest people in his company. That year, he opened a factory in what is now part of Pittsburgh. Heinz offered tours of the factory. The tours also showed buyers how clean the factory was. People came from around the world to take the tour. Each received Heinz company product samples and a pickle pin to take home.

A restored Heinz delivery wagon is on display at the Senator John Heinz History Center in Pittsburgh.

Making Waves

In 1905, Heinz **incorporated** the company. This meant that the company would be legally considered an individual, separate from the owner. Incorporating had many advantages. One was that if anything happened to Heinz, the company could continue without him. Another advantage was that Heinz could give **shares** of the business to other people, such as his children.

Throughout his life, quality continued to be very important to Heinz. In the early 1900s, there were no laws regulating food quality. But Heinz worked hard to make sure each of his products met his own high standards. He wanted his customers to have the best products he could make. And he believed buyers should receive the same quality in every Heinz product they purchased.

Heinz thought other companies should have to live up to these same high standards. Together with his son Howard, Heinz began fighting for a food quality law. On June 30, 1906, President Theodore Roosevelt signed the Pure Food and Drug Act. Food companies now had to make sure their products met certain quality standards.

The H.J. Heinz & Company board of directors in 1909. Heinz (seated at desk) was the company's president. His sons Howard (far left) and Clarence (second from right) were also on the board.

All in the Family

Heinz company produced quality products throughout Heinz's life. On May 14, 1919, Heinz died at the age of 74. Heinz's son Howard took over as president of the company. Previously, Howard had been the US Food **Administrator** in Pennsylvania. In that job, he had continued to fight for high standards in the food industry.

Heinz company grew quickly under Howard. When he took over, it had 6,500 workers in 25 factories around the world. In the 1920s, the company purchased more land and opened more factories. Howard traveled often to oversee the work at factories across the globe.

These efforts paid off during the **Great Depression**. Many companies were going broke. But Heinz company had no **debt** and continued to expand. It even started making new products, such as soup and baby food.

In 1937, Heinz company opened a factory in Ohio. It would become the largest ketchup factory in the country. By 1939, H.J. Heinz Company was worth more than $100 million. Howard remained president of the company until he died in 1941.

Howard (right) with Pennsylvania Senator George Wharton Pepper

Next of Kin

Howard's son Henry John Heinz II soon took over the company when his father died. Henry John II went by the name Jack. At a young age, Jack began working at Heinz company as a pickle salter. He went on to work in every department, from canning to cleaning. After college, Jack went to Australia to open a Heinz company plant there. It became the country's biggest food-processing plant.

In his first few years as president and CEO, Jack doubled the company's sales. He started companies owned by Heinz company in other countries, including Venezuela and Japan. These companies made **versions** of Heinz company products for local buyers. Jack also expanded the Heinz company by buying several other food companies. Jack stepped down as president and CEO in 1966.

After Jack stepped down, R. Burt Gookin took over as the company's

Ore Ida Foods was one brand the Heinz company bought under Jack's leadership.

CEO. Gookin was a longtime Heinz company employee. He was the first nonfamily member to become CEO.

H.J. Heinz Company continued to do well under Gookin's leadership. By 1972, it had made more than $1 billion in sales. Gookin retired in 1979 and Anthony O'Reilly became CEO. O'Reilly had been an executive at Heinz company for many years. As CEO, he helped the company grow even more.

Although no longer the company's president, Jack remained on the board until his death in 1987.

Heinz Today

Over the next 40 years, Heinz company continued to build its empire. It added more sauces, dressings, and toppings to its product line. In 2015, the company **merged** with Kraft Foods to become the Kraft Heinz Company.

Kraft is best known for making macaroni and cheese. But it also makes other popular foods. These include Jell-O brand gelatin, Planters brand nuts, and Oscar Mayer brand hot dogs.

Today, Kraft Heinz is the third-largest food and drink company in North America. It is the fifth-largest in the world. Its products can be found in 200 countries around the world. Eight of its brands each make more than $1 billion each year.

For more than 100 years, Heinz company products have set the standard for quality foods. What started as a young boy's small door-to-door business has grown into a successful international corporation. Heinz's products are found in kitchens all over the world, especially his **iconic** ketchup. The next time you are in a restaurant, check the labels on the ketchup bottles. They will most likely say Heinz!

In 1968, Heinz company started selling ketchup in small packets.
Today, 11 billion packets are sold each year.

Timeline

1844	Henry John "H.J." Heinz was born in Pittsburgh, Pennsylvania, on October 11.
1852	Heinz began selling vegetables from his mother's garden to his neighbors.
1869	Heinz married Sarah Sloan "Sallie" Young. He formed Heinz, Noble & Company with L. Clarence Noble.
1875	Heinz filed for bankruptcy on December 17.
1876	Heinz began managing F. and J. Heinz Company, a business owned by his brother and cousin. He launched ketchup as part of their product line.
1888	Heinz bought F. and J. Heinz Company and renamed it H.J. Heinz Company.
1893	Heinz went to the Chicago World's Fair. He gave fairgoers a souvenir to encourage them to visit his booth.
1898	Heinz opened a new factory in what is now part of Pittsburgh. He let people tour the building.
1919	Heinz died on May 14 at age 74.

Ketchup Facts

How much do you know about Heinz ketchup?
Here are some fun facts that may surprise you.

Each year, Heinz sells more than 650 million bottles of Heinz ketchup.

Each Heinz ketchup bottle cap has a code on it. The company can use the code to track the bottle everywhere it goes.

Heinz company tests each batch of ketchup for thickness. When poured out of a glass bottle, it should move at 0.028 miles per hour (0.045 kmh). If it pours faster, the batch is discarded.

From 2000 to 2006, Heinz company sold EZ Squirt ketchup. EZ Squirt tasted like regular ketchup, but it came in different colors. The colors included green, purple, blue, and pink.

Heinz uses more than 2 million tons (1.8 million t) of tomatoes each year. That's more than any other company in the world!

Glossary

administrator - a person who manages an operation, a department, or an office.

American Civil War - from 1861 to 1865. A war between the United States of America and the Confederate States of America.

bankruptcy - the state of having been legally declared unable to pay a debt.

brickyard - a place where bricks are made.

debt (DEHT) - something owed to someone, especially money.

economic - relating to the production and use of goods and services.

Great Depression - the period from 1929 to 1942 of worldwide economic trouble. There was little buying or selling, and many people could not find work.

iconic - widely recognized and well established.

immigrant - a person who enters another country to live.

incorporated - formed into a legal corporation.

merge - to combine or blend, such as when two or more companies combine into one business.

preservative - an additive used to protect against decay, discoloration, or spoilage.

pulp - the soft, juicy part of a fruit.

sauerkraut - finely chopped cabbage that is salted and allowed to sour.

share - one of the equal parts into which the ownership of a company is divided.

slogan - a word or a phrase used to express a position, a stand, or a goal.

souvenir - something that is kept as a reminder of something.

stock market - a place where stocks and bonds, which represent parts of businesses, are bought and sold.

version - a different form or type of an original.

Websites

To learn more about Food Dudes, visit **abdobooklinks.com**. These links are routinely monitored and updated to provide the most current information available.

Index